BUSES OF NORTH STAFFORDSHIRE

BUSES OF NORTH STAFFORDSHIRE

TIM MACHIN

AMBERLEY

First published 2021

Amberley Publishing
The Hill, Stroud
Gloucestershire, GL5 4EP

www.amberley-books.com

Copyright © Tim Machin, 2021

The right of Tim Machin to be identified as
the Authors of this work has been asserted in
accordance with the Copyright, Designs and
Patents Act 1988.

ISBN 978 1 4456 9950 9 (print)
ISBN 978 1 4456 9951 6 (ebook)

British Library Cataloguing in Publication Data.
A catalogue record for this book is available from
the British Library.

Origination by Amberley Publishing.
Printed in the UK.

Introduction

The Author

Born in Shrewsbury in 1961, I moved (unknowingly) to the North Staffordshire mining village of Brown Edge when I was three months old, from that point onwards I started a relationship with the PSV operations of North Staffordshire. Dad was a travelling salesman for many years and Mum didn't drive, so our only transport was by bus. School trips to Chester Zoo and such faraway places were always done by an immaculate Bedford, SB, VAM or VAL in the green/cream livery of Turners. Trips into nearby towns were either by Turners (to Hanley) or PMT (Burslem, Newcastle or Leek). Shortly before my ninth birthday we moved to Kidsgrove, served by the often down at heel dull maroon/lilac buses of Stoniers. We lived on the main A50 trunk road, and the front bedroom over our newsagents afforded a bird's eye view of all manner of interesting vehicles – not least PMT's fleet of noisy Daimler Roadliners. By the mid-70s I was in possession of a camera, and some of those early shots, captured on the very odd sized Agfa CNS-2 rapid film, feature in this volume.

On starting secondary school, I met someone else with the same interest in buses and so commenced my life-long friendship with Martyn Hearson (who has kindly contributed a number of photos to this book). We embarked on days out bus spotting, first by public transport. Both having left school on the same day, we abandoned our A Levels in favour of careers with the well-known independent Berresfords Motors. Once we had obtained our driving licenses, our bus spotting days out were by car – either my Hillman Minx or Martyn's Imp. Our long-suffering girlfriends (both of whom must secretly have been impressed as they later became our wives, and still are!) were taken to minute Welsh villages, seaside resorts in inclement weather and all sorts of places they'd never heard of.

The interest in buses has remained to this day, with a particular affection for the smaller operator. My career has taken me on a journey around these operators; from years spent as a schedules clerk for PMT; transport manager for a variety of independents; driver for PMT, Knotty, Berresfords, Stoniers, Stevensons and many others. Even during my twenty years as a signalman on the rail network, my first love was buses, and other than for a two year break in the late '70s, I've always worked, even if only on a part-time basis, in the PSV industry.

The Book

Well, where to begin. A suggestion by Connor Stait of Amberley Publishing started me thinking – could I find the requisite 180 photos to tell in part a story of PSV operations in North Staffordshire? After months of sifting through my own photos, and those of many other people, the issue became what to leave out rather than what to include.

I have deliberately avoided too many photos from PMT, Stevensons and Berresfords, as in recent years each of those has been the subject of separate publications.

My journey starts in the early 1970s and comes up to date. I have tried to include as much variety, both in vehicle types and geography, as possible. You will also find a few operators based outside North Staffordshire, but all have provided either local bus or works and schools' services into the area. For many of the smaller operator's, bus service work was only a small part of their operations and we will see many contract and private hire/tour coaches as well as service buses. A number of PSVs have traditionally gone on to an 'afterlife' providing private transport for workers, dance troupes, fishing clubs etc. and some of these are also included.

Geographically, I have drawn an invisible line across the county, including Uttoxeter and Stafford, working northwards to the county boundaries with Derbyshire, Cheshire and Shropshire.

The industrialised area within North Staffordshire consists mainly of Stoke-on-Trent and 'The Potteries' – a sprawling of six Victorian era towns, once a busy industrial area, with steel works, pottery manufacturers and coal miners as its main employers, all of which, bar a handful of small pottery works, have vanished over the past thirty years. Newcastle-Under-Lyme, Leek and Cheadle were all homes to mills producing, among other items, paper and clothing for well-known high-street brands. The loss of these industries has obviously removed the need for 'workers services' provided by many of the operators herein.

North Staffordshire as an area was unusual as it had no local authority operators. Services were provided in the main part by former BET company PMT, which by the 70s, of course, was part of the National Bus Company. Pre-deregulation, the area had settled since the early 1960s with few operators coming or going, but 1986 changed all that. PMT, an early example of a manager buyout, launched vicious attacks (often very wastefully) on pretty much every small provider of bus services within the Stoke-on-Trent area. Big old established names vanished. By the late 1990s only Procters remained from pre-deregulation days, still operating their Hanley–Leek service 16, basically as they had since the 1920s. PMT had changed hands again to become part of the Badgerline Group, later First Bus. Rural area services were lost, as second car ownership became normal, and cross subsidisation of routes went out of fashion. Big operators, in the main, were happy to de-register anything which ran at either marginal or no profit, in the hope that the county council would then invite tenders to run the service – sometimes it happened, but in other cases many communities lost the 'village bus' forever.

The operators featured range from the immaculately presented fleets of Copeland's, Paul's, Plants etc. to those who appear to run on a shoestring budget, and they, like their vehicles, had better remain nameless! Such operators, however, all help provide variety, their often-unusual vehicles covering low mileages providing school transport. Obviously in the space available I have not been able to include every operator, and many are not included simply because the only views I have failed to make my final selection. There are also a great many smaller operators from the 1970s and 1980s for whom no photos seem to be available anywhere. The final choice of photos is very much a personal one, touching, I hope, on most aspects of bus/coach operations in the area over the last forty-five or so years. I have tried to feature a variety of different types from minibuses to double deckers, to traditional and modern and coaches of many types and styles, hopefully providing a few things to cater for everyone and maybe a few forgotten memories will be returned.

I would like to give special thanks to my wife, Jill, for typing my illegible comments and captions, and for spending most of 2019 with boxes and piles of photographs all around the house. Wherever possible, any photos which aren't mine have been credited to their takers, whom I would like to thank for making them available to me. In some cases, with photos I have purchased many years ago, I have been unable to trace the photographer – if I have unknowingly used your photo without permission please accept my apologies. Information has come from my own notes, many bus handbooks, PSV circle publications etc. and operators themselves. Any mistakes are mine and mine alone. Final thanks to Connor and the team at Amberley for their encouragement.

AHD 995R, Ford R1014 Plaxton C45F, owned by Jim Stonier of Shelton at the time of this 1992 photo, had previously been in the fleet of Durber, Graham's Coaches of Talke from 1986 to 1990. After use by Stonier, it moved briefly to Zamir of Burton-on-Trent, then returned to Stoke-on-Trent to Copeland's, Meir, by July 1993. It was scrapped at Meir June 1994. In this view it's having a wash/brush up in the yard of Knotty Bus, Chesterton.

Bassetts Coachways of Tittensor bought this neat little twenty-seat Caetano-bodied Toyota Coaster new in June 1988. Enjoying a visit to North Wales three years later, it's seen at the Builder Street West Coach park in Llandudno. Bassetts had started out as hauliers and only moved into PSV operation after the war, buying a number of Foden coaches new. The company remains in business, still operating from its original – but much enlarged – premises on the A34, though PSV operations were abandoned in 2003.

L561 ASU, an ex-military spec Dennis Javelin/Wadham Stringer Vanguard II B70F, arrived with Transport Direct of Bramshall in August 2017 from the well-known fleet of White Bus Services, Winkfield Row, Berkshire. As normal with Transport Direct and the closely associated operation of JST, Uttoxeter, the bus remained in its previous operator's livery, complete with fleet names. It gave twelve months reliable, economical service over a fairly demanding school contract route to Cheadle, via Alton, and was a favourite of mine to drive. Its good performance on hills, excellent visibility and light steering, brakes and gear change making it a pleasure to drive. It was sadly scrapped in August 2018 on the expiry of its MOT.

GAZ 7117 was a Leyland Leopard with an interesting history. New to PMT as XBF 60S with Duple Dominant Express bodywork, it later passed to Frontrunner Buses. It received its new Willowbrook Warrior body in 1992 later passing, via Stevensons, to Sherratt (County Bus) of Seighford. By February 1999 it had passed to Goldstraw of Leek, trading as Aimee's and TaxiCo, receiving it's fifth registration number, having been PIJ 660, YYJ 955, and VOV 936S at various stages.

Another member of the Aimee's fleet was A102 RGE, bought from Kent CC late in 2001, along with similar A105 RGE. Both were examples of the well-built and comparatively rare Dennis Dorchester with Alexander TE bodywork. Both had been upseated with three and two seating to give a sixty-five-seat capacity. The Dorchester was Dennis' answer to the Leyland Tiger, featuring a Gardner 6HLXCT engine and sold mostly in Scotland. It gave around five years' service before sadly being vandalised and scrapped.

A purpose-built school bus, YN54 VVP, a Turkish-built BMC1100FE with sixty-one seats. Simply and ruggedly built, featuring a noisy and harsh front-mounted four-cylinder Cummins B Series engine and Allison automatic gearbox. The vehicle was reminiscent of a 1960s Ford, with steel suspension and a very old-fashioned driving position. Acquired by Transport Direct/JST from Wilfreida Beehive in April 2016, it gave around eighteen months sporadic service before being dumped, unloved, in a corner of the yard. Once again it was never repaired.

Glebe Street bridge adjacent to Stoke Station has claimed many victims over the years with its 10-foot 3-inch height restriction. From PMT's large fleet of Nationals, some would fit, others wouldn't. Here in the relaxed pre-deregulations days of the early 1980s, an 11.3 m example has successfully passed beneath the bridge en route from Werrington to Stoke on service 154.

Twenty-five years on from the previous photo and buses and services have changed more than anyone could have imagined. PMT, from being a nearly 500 vehicle operator, had seen its fleet more than halved and only had two operational depots. Once again Glebe Street bridge provides the backdrop for the standard minibus of the late 1990s/early 2000s, a Plaxton Beaver II-bodied Mercedes Vario R245 ERE.

The Leyland National found a few independents in North Staffordshire willing to give it a try. The first was Stonier of Goldenhill, recently absorbed into the Berresford Group. In October 1978, SCO 427L, a forty-six-seat dual-entrance example arrived from Plymouth. Only five years old, the Plymouth examples were among the first to come onto the second-hand market. SCO proved unreliable in service with Stonier and its complex modern engineering was unfamiliar to the mechanics used to working on Leyland PD3s. Its appearances in service were few and far between, but it's seen here in early 1979 in Hanley Bus Station. Withdrawn soon after, plans to re-engine it never happened and it was left to rot at the depot until 1987.

One of the more stylish attempts at a minibus was the MCW Metrorider. Following the closure of MCW the design was taken on and updated by Optare. A late example, R393 ERE, was one of a small batch delivered to PMT in September 1997. It is seen here in Leek Bus Station wearing the PMT privatised livery of red/yellow but with 'First' fleetnames, ready to depart on an off-peak journey which would take it across the Potteries to its destination of the University Village of Keele. It saw ten years in service.

One of the best known and distinctive fleets of the post-deregulation era was that of Knotty Bus. Its life may have been fairly short, lasting around eleven years, but many fascinating vehicles were operated in that time. The first service bus in the fleet was BWN 462K, an AEC Reliance 6MU2R/Marshall, which arrived from a small South Wales independent in 1990. Looking very smart about to depart for the AEC Rally in that year, it was to see less than a year in service due to bodywork issues. The idea was to rebuild it, but sadly, it never happened, and it went for scrap in 1994.

Few vehicles, other than AECs, carried Knotty livery and only one Bedford, KPV 830V, a Duple Dominant II Express-bodied YMT which unusually had a two-speed axle, making it very pleasant to drive, with a good spread of power for a Bedford. It was normally used on a variety of service and contract work. It is seen here on a damp morning in 1993 awaiting its departure time from Norton to Hanley. After use by Knotty it went to an East Anglia operator for use as a driver trainer and was last taxed in 1996.

MWA 839P, new to National Travel, had arrived with Knotty Bus by 1992. A lovely bus to drive, smooth and powerful, its manual door meant most of its time was occupied on contract or private hire work. Parked up for the evening, it's in Cheadle outside the premises of Millmoors body builders.

One of my favourite vehicles to drive, JWO 891L, arrived with Knotty in 1990 following the absorption of the business of Halls Coaches of Rock End. The AEC Reliance 6MU4R had been new as one of a pair supplied to Edmunds of Rassau. It was a good performing and very economical to use bus, with a six-speed constant mesh manual gearbox, and carrying the Express version of Plaxton's Panorama Elite III bodywork. Another early 1990s view sees it waiting time at the Rose and Crown Biddulph Moor on the hourly service to Hanley. Last taxed in 1993, the end came for it when a tree destroyed its bodywork during a storm.

S. Turner kept a small fleet at their High Lane garage in Brown Edge. Unusually, two different liveries were used, coaches in two greens and cream, and buses (all double deckers) in Tudor Maroon and Cream. LVT 699V, No. 8, a Leyland Fleetline/ Northern Counties was the final new purchase and is seen here departing Hanley Bus Station for its home village in 1987. It is pleasing to report the bus has survived in preservation with Martyn Hearson.

Due to a vehicle shortage in the early 1980s PMT bought a number of time expired Bristol RE saloons from Bristol Omnibus. The only curved screen example, EHU 379K, was numbered 180 and put to use at Burslem Garage. It's seen here on Shelton New Road, Basford, on the 324 service bound for Alsager from Hanley via Newcastle. It was never repainted, and it was operated from June to August 1980.

Stevensons, based at Spath, near Uttoxeter, operated a very traditional fleet of buses and coaches in a distinctive yellow and black livery. Service, private hire and contracts were operated. This former City of Oxford short-length AEC Renown, DFC 365D, is on contract duties in this 1977 view taken in Church Street, Stoke-on-Trent outside the Market Hall, which was later destroyed by fire.

Another vehicle to make it into preservation is KRE 279P, an 11.3 m Leyland National owned by PMT. Awaiting its next turn of duty in Newcastle Bus Station in the mid-1980s carrying its distinctive blue/yellow 'Silverdale Shuttle' livery, it looks very uncared for. It can now be seen at local transport events fully restored into Poppy Red all-over livery by owner Dave Wright.

Trent Travel, based in Cheadle, are a comparative newcomer, operations commencing in 2014. Ready to operate a school contract to its hometown, seen in the morning sun in Leek Bus Station in July 2019, is a comparatively rare Mercedes Benz 0404 with fifty-three-seat Hispano Coachwork, LEZ 7045. The vehicle came from Squirrells in Suffolk in 2016 and was scrapped in September 2019.

Phil Smith Travel are based at Stramshall near Uttoxeter and operate an immaculate fleet of coaches and minibuses on a variety of work. NIB 3261, a DAF SB3000/Van Hool, is picking up passengers from Blyth Bridge High School, shortly after purchase in 2014. Soon after this photo was taken it was resprayed in all-over white, and departed the fleet in the summer of 2019, passing to A1 Travel, also of Uttoxeter.

One of the best presented fleets in North Staffordshire is that of Paul's Coaches, Newchapel. Paul commenced operations in his own name on the retirement of his father, Graham Durber, who traded as Graham's. Wearing the distinctive blue livery is Dennis Javelin F622 SAY, carrying the fairly uncommon low driver LS3200 version of Plaxton's Paramount III Coachwork.

Stanways Coaches, based at various times in North Staffordshire and just over the border in South Cheshire, have in recent years adopted a distinctive red/orange/white livery. A fairly elderly but tidy fleet is operated. Dennis Javelin F639 SAY had been new to Coppenhalls of Sandbach and joined the Stanways fleet from them in 2003. Re-seated to C70F for schools' duties, for a few years it carried the registration BIG 7013, reverting to its original registration shortly before disposal in 2016. Duple 320 bodywork was carried.

LWO 316E, a Leyland Leopard PSU4/3RT Plaxton C43F, joined the Berresfords of Cheddleton fleet in 1979 from Jones Aberbeeg. Its short length made it a very handy vehicle for rural services and contracts. It's seen in Hartington on a sunny spring morning in 1985, ready to depart for Leek on the Wednesday/Saturday only service 463, at that time part of the 'Peak Pathfinder' network of services. I always found it an enjoyable vehicle to drive, though it could be hard work with its manual gearbox, manual door operation and no power steering. It put in seven years' reliable service and was scrapped when the Berresfords business passed to PMT in 1987.

Another market day only service was the 184, Cheadle–Freehay–Uttoxeter, this time operated on Wednesdays only. In the early 1990s it was operated under tender by Knotty Bus, in whose ownership we see 12 m AEC Reliance/Plaxton Supreme ANA 8T making the tight turn at Hollington Church, driven by Kevin Staples. The coach, hardly the most suitable vehicle to the route, had been new to Godfrey Abbott, arriving at Knotty in 1990 from Lancaster City Transport.

With a backdrop of the ruins of Croxden Abbey in June 2019, we see former Wints Coaches SG52 VFO, Mercedes 0814 Plaxton Cheetah, now with Trent Travel of Cheadle, operating a schools' contract from Hollington to Rocester.

Byrnes of Leek were a subsidiary of the Berresfords Motors Group and operated from Buxton Road Garage in Leek. FAX 295C, a Leyland Leopard Harrington Grenadier, had arrived from Jones, Aberbeeg, in 1978 and lasted around four years. Byrnes operations involved some of the most testing hills and lanes in the Moorlands, as can be seen here. (Photographer – unknown)

Better known as coach operators, Boydens of Winkhill operated three Leyland Leopard service buses back in the early 1990s. Former Southdown Northern Counties-bodied PUF 171H was bought in 1983. It is seen the same year in Leek Bus Station on layover before setting out on service via the Ashbourne Road and Grindon for its home village. Boydens commenced operations pre-war but expansion to larger vehicles only came following the closure of Smiths Tours, Waterhouses, in 1982. The company closed in 2006, but it's pleasing to say that operations restarted in 2019.

Q609 FVT, a Bedford YLQ Willowbrook B45 had been supplied new to Douglas Corporation Transport as MAN 139B. It arrived at Berresfords in 1985 carrying the registration number PDJ 732W. A new reg. of FWB 181V was issued, but on presentation for MOT, prior to entering service, the registration details were refused. Eventually it was re-registered again as seen here in this 1987 view at Longton Bus Station.

Pooles Coachways of Alsagers bank was another traditional independent which could trace its roots back to the 1920s. For many years a livery of maroon and white was used, the areas of white increasing throughout the 1960s and 1970s. By the mid-1980s the proprietors wished to retire; if it weren't for the unfortunate death of Jim Berresford the business would have become part of the Berresford Empire. As it was, it passed to the McCready Group from Newcastle, and a white/blue livery adapted. One of the vehicles so painted was VBX 222L, a Plaxton Derwent-bodied Leyland Leopard, disposed of by its original owners, West Wales, in 1982. Looking very grubby, it's seen in Hanley Bus Station in 1988. Pooles eventually closed, after further changes of ownership, following maintenance problems at the end of the 1990s.

YP52 BPK, one of three Optare Alero twelve-seaters supplied to Wardle of Norton under Stoke-on-Trent City Council sponsorship. Once a provider of disabled minibuses as Jacks of Norton, Wardle grew in the early years of the twenty-first century to become one of the most prominent service operators in the city. Acquired by Arriva in December 2010, the operations had quietly floundered by 2014.

Ron Eyre, trading as Robin Hood Coaches, is still operating to this day with a fleet of immaculate green Bova coaches from his rural depot at Rushton Spencer, near Leek. A sharp contrast to today's vehicles is 233 JRE, a 1955 Bedford SBO Duple Midland service bus, acquired in early 1971 from Corrington–Dewhurst of Ecclestone, Lancashire. Employed mainly on works services to various mills in Leek, it was still on fleet strength in 1980.

Another elderly vehicle still in use in 1980 was Stevensons of Uttoxeter 1500 WJ, the first production Leyland Leopard. Sadly scrapped soon after this photograph was taken, the distinctive rear view of its Weymann Fanfare body is taken under the railway bridge at Longton Town Hall. It is operating a works service. Only two Weymann Fanfares survive in preservation – an AEC Reliance and a Leyland Tiger Cub.

199 NEH, a Plaxton Consort IV-bodied Bedford SB3. Another long-lived vehicle retaining its petrol engine until the end. New in July 1960 to Percy Stoddard, Greenhill Garage, Cheadle, it was finally withdrawn with severe bodywork problems at the end of 1983. Stoddards traded as 'Swallow Coaches' and their navy blue/pale fawn fleet carried a swallow emblem. Some bus service work was undertaken and NEH was a regular performer on the Fridays-only Hollington–Cheadle service.

473 FCG, a 1962 AEC Reliance/Park Royal C49F, had arrived with Sergent, Wrinehill, from Alder Valley in 1976. Here it is at the depot around four years later along with 4872 DF, LTE 262C and CFM 444H. Sergent provided mainly schools and works services. Operations had ceased by the mid-1980s.

At the turn of the 1970s, Elkes Biscuits of Uttoxeter operated a pair of AEC Regent III/Weyman Lowbridge double deckers. KYY 516 had been new to London Transport as fleet number RLH16 in June 1950. They were replaced at Elkes by a trio of Bedford VALs and sold for scrap. Against all odds, one survived in a Uttoxeter scrapyard for over thirty-five years until the yard was cleared.

F158 XYG, a Northern Counties-bodied Leyland Olympian had been new to Yorkshire Rider in November 1988. By March 1999 it had become number 890 in the PMT fleet, allocated to Cheadle depot, by this time located on Brookhouse Industrial Estate, the location of this photograph. Its stay with PMT was quite short, but happily it appears to have survived and was last taxed in 2015.

LAK 296G, one of a batch of similar MCW-bodied Leyland PDR1/3 Atlanteans new to Bradford Corporation in 1968. It arrived in Staffordshire from West Yorkshire PTE and joined the W. Stonier & Sons fleet, at Tunstall, by early 1982. It's seen here, turned from Roebuck Street into Leek Road, Stoke, soon after entering service, bound, despite the destination display, for Bentilee on service 71. It was withdrawn and sold for scrap in late 1984.

Heading for Chester from Hanley in the early 1990s, Midland Redline, formerly Midland Red North Dennis Dominator/East Lancs H806 AHA, is operating the former Crosville service C84. Its seventy-six-seat capacity appearing unnecessary for this particular journey.

An unusual little bus, ELZ 2972, had been new as F599 OYX in August 1988. Beneath its thirty-seat Wright bodywork lay a Leyland 9-13R chassis, more commonly used as a basis for light commercial vehicles. Despite wearing full Clowes Coaches livery, including route branding for the lengthy 458 Longnor–Hanley service, it's actually operated by Phil Clowes (Phil's Travel) and was taking a break from its normal weekday Leek–Ipstones–Cheadle service. Phil's Travel commenced operations in 2003 but ceased a few years later.

Another type which had little impact on the PSV market was the Fiat/Iveco 70.14. This Reeves-Burgess twenty-nine-seater carrying Plaxton's demonstration livery was new to Rumplan Ltd of Newcastle-Under-Lyme, trading as Roseville Taxis. It was under a year old when pictured at the Staffordshire County Showground, in summer 1992, in the company of two vehicles from the Hollinshead of Scholar Green fleet.

The Dennis Dart proved a best seller as a bus, but as a coach few were sold. N983 BHE was one of a handful carrying Wadham Stringer Winchester bodies. Owned by the author, it was in operation for Stanways at the time of the photograph and was a delightful little thing to drive. After use by Stanways I sold it to JST at Uttoxeter. One of a pair new to Rotherham Borough Council in August 1995, it was eventually sold for conversion to a motor caravan.

Wints Coaches of Butterton had a penchant for the unusual so it's no surprise to find L964 NWW in their fleet. New to Wallace Arnold in 1994, it was one of only a handful of Volvo B6R chassis to receive coach bodies. Disposed of by WA at an early age, it was twenty years old by the time it arrived at Wints. Withdrawn in 2016 it appears to have found further use until the end of 2017.

55 CAA was a late 1961 Duple Britannia-bodied AEC Reliance from the fleet of Bill Hall of Foxlowe Garage Rock End Biddulph Moor. In order to seat forty-three passengers, the final batch of Britannia bodies were built to a 31-foot 10-inch length instead of 30-foot. It remained in service with Halls until 1980, having arrived in June 1977 from Kuhlenz of Shirebrook.

AFN 598B was a rather distinctive Park Royal C49F-bodied AEC Reliance, new to East Kent in 1964, arriving at Berresfords in 1978 along with identical AFN 599B. Waiting time outside the old Hanley Baths in Lichfield Street, the area behind it is now part of the new and totally inadequate bus station. AFN gave three years' service before being scrapped.

Procters UFA 698R, AEC Reliance Duple Dominant II C57F, was usually kept to contract and private hire work but is pictured here in Hanley Bus Station. It was the penultimate of several Reliances bought by Procters.

GSU 7T, a 1978 Plaxton Supreme III-bodied AEC Reliance, new to Hutchinson of Overtown. Modernised with a Mk IV front, it joined the Boyden of Winkhill fleet in 1985 from Flear of Middlesborough. Obviously a good purchase, it lasted for over sixteen years with Boydens. Here in Uttoxeter it awaits its passengers for All Saints School, at Church Leigh, to return from their swimming lessons.

Uttoxeter Leisure Centre is the backdrop for this 1994 view of H313 WUA, No. 33 in the Stevensons fleet, a Leyland Swift, with Reeves Burgess Harrier bodywork, new to Pennine of Garsgrove as one of a pair. Disappointed with the quality and after sales backup, they were sold by Pennine when less than a year old. Both joined the Stevensons fleet, which at one time boasted the largest fleet of Swifts in the UK. No. 33 was one of the nicer Swifts to drive.

BX11 HHG, A BMC 850 thirty-five-seater, supplied new to Warringtons of Ilam. A popular and well-liked midi coach, it has recently been repainted into Warringtons traditional colours. Established in the 1920s and now in the hands of the third generation of the family, Warringtons are the oldest established family-run operator in North Staffordshire. Over the years, service work has dwindled in favour of private hire, tours and school contracts. (Photo by Tony Wilson)

YRE 529Y, a Mercedes 409 with Midland Commercials sixteen-seater body, operated by Swift Mini Coaches. The vehicle transferred ownership, along with the company, from the late PMT inspector Ray Bostock, to Frank Booth of Duke Street Fenton. It remained in service until Swift Mini Coaches ceased trading in 2003. It was then dumped at the Foxfield Railway site at Blythe Bridge, where it remained for a few years before disappearing without trace.

YX04 AWU is pictured at Plants Cheadle depot. A Mercedes 084D with Autobus Classique Nouvelle bodywork seating twenty-nine, it was supplied new to Plants, an operator dating back to the 1960s. Plants specialise in high-class small vehicle travel, keeping an immaculate fleet of high-spec up-to-date vehicles for schools and corporate work.

P120 XCN from the JST/Transport Direct fleet was a 1997 Volvo B10M-55 Alexander B49F purchased from Lavender of Shipley in 2012. As with many vehicles in the fleet it kept the colours of its previous operator, with just a paper sticker in a nearside window indicating ownership. It's pictured here in 2015, driven by Alan Challinor at Draycott in the Clay, working a Uttoxeter schools' contract. The Bramshall-based operator is basically a provider of home to schools' transport, though at the time of this photo P120 XCN was a regular vehicle on the Wednesdays-only market day service from Leigh to Uttoxeter.

NIL 8261, new as F709 PAY to Pullmanor of Camberwell, is a fine V8-powered Mercedes 0303 integral fifty-three-seater that joined the Wints fleet in October 1997. At one point the fleet contained no fewer than four of these rare coaches. NIL is pictured in 2014 at the Gladstone Museum in Longton. It gave Wints twenty-one years' service almost to the day before sadly catching fire in Onecote one morning, while returning to the garage. Wints stopped operating at the end of 2018 but have kept similar coach F705 PAY for preservation.

MRF 232L was a Bedford VASS with Duple Vista 25 bodywork seating twenty-nine passengers. New to Roy Cooper of Elkstone in 1972, it was the first 'real' bus operated by Colin Wint, who had commenced operations in 1974 from Wetton with a new Ford Transit YBF 962M. By the time MRF entered the fleet, operations were based in a new purpose-built garage and bungalow at Butterton. Throughout its stay it retained its original green/orange/cream colours.

A long-standing member of the fleet of Sergents of Wrinehill, CFM 444H had arrived there from Marsh of Plumpton in July 1977. New in August 1969 to Taylor of Chester this Ford R192 carried a stylish Duple Viceroy 32 body. It remained with Sergent until operation ceased. Pictured here owned by C & H dance troupe, Chesterton, in 1991, with the author at the wheel, it had suffered a broken windscreen and was scrapped shortly afterwards.

This little Trojan thirteen-seater 80EKC, new in 1959, was a valuable addition to the Smiths Tours fleet from Waterhouses. Employed for several years carrying first contractors, and then workers to the new Cement Works in the village, its noisy three-cylinder Perkins engine proved unbreakable. It lasted for over ten years from its arrival in May 1961 before sale to Roy Middling of Chesterton, Staffordshire, in whose blue/white (probably unpainted since Smiths days) it's seen in here.

A Knotty Bus line up in the overspill yard in the mid-1990s. No. 19, CYA 181J AEC Reliance/Plaxton Derwent B47F; No. 23, JPF 103K AEC Swift/Alexander 'W' Type DP48F; No. 22 VCW 598Y Dennis Lancet/Marshall B53F; No. 3 KVE 909P AEC Reliance/Plaxton Supreme C49F (Paramount front).

OFY 658, a charming Reading-bodied Karrier with seating for fourteen, was already very outdated when it arrived with Ivor J. Lucas of Hollington in 1972, from Bullock and France of Southport, to whom it had been new in 1958. It had a fairly short stay in the fleet and had gone by 1974 for private use. Last taxed at the end of 1984, it is assumed to have been scrapped.

This view, taken inside Berresfords Garage at Cheddleton in June 1987 shortly after takeover by PMT, shows Leyland Leopard SJA 370J, Bristol VR HRE 529N, and Stonier's AEC Reliance NPT 992M, all receiving attention. All three vehicles went on to see service outside North Staffordshire. SJA went to Silcox, Pembroke Dock, HRE joined PMT Red-Rider fleet in Yorkshire and NPT went to Merlyns at Skewen.

A second-hand purchase by Warringtons of Ilam was OPT 463J, Bedford YRQ/ Willowbrook 001 DP45F. New to Scarlet Band, West Carnforth, in July 1971 it was more or less in Warrington colours when it arrived and so wasn't repainted. In this view from around 1982 it is in Hartington, famous for its cheese, having no doubt worked in from Ashbourne, just over the border in Derbyshire. (Photo J. P. Bennett)

Pooles Coachways of Alsagers Bank bought DRF 133E new in April 1967 and operated it for over twenty years. It's heading along Bradwell Lane towards Porthill on a schools' service towards the end of its life. Bodywork was by Willowbrook to their 'Motorway Express' design, featuring long window bays, forced air ventilation, coach seats, luggage boot and a sloping rear dome.

UTX 727S, in addition to finding fame in the tv series *Peak Practice* this ex-Cynon Valley Leyland National arrived in Stoke-on-Trent from Camms of Nottingham. Parked at Fenton in this late 1990s view, it was a short-term member of the Countrywide fleet of Frank Booth, where it was used on contract work and the Wednesdays-only service 184 from Cheadle to Uttoxeter.

SN04 GBZ, a Mercedes 0814D twenty-four-seater with bodywork by KVC conversions, was new to Moffatt, Kirkpatrick Fleming, but is seen in 2013 with Phil Smith Travel amid icy surroundings at Greatgate. It is operating the Fridays-only Staffs. County Council service to Cheadle.

MFA 29V was the second Caetano Alpha-bodied Ford R1114 supplied new to Bill Stanton, trading as BC Travel. This photo shows it in Amsterdam in the summer of 1980 working on hire to Midland Travel Limited. The coach was short-lived with BC Travel, passing to Rogers of Longside when only six months old. Bill was one of the great characters of PSV operation in the Potteries area but sadly passed away four years ago. His legacy lives on with his son, Keith, who is trading very successfully as Stantons of Stoke (Going My Way Ltd). (Photo Frans Angevaare)

VVT 577X was the second of a non-identical pair of Leyland Leopards supplied new to Graham Durber of Talke in January 1982. It was only the second 11 m Leopard chassis to carry the new Plaxton Supreme V body and is presented in its usual immaculate order at Clough Hall Sports Centre, Kidsgrove. (Photo Martyn Hearson)

B250 HUX, a late model Ford R1115 with Plaxton Paramount body, was supplied new to Jones of Market Drayton, just over the border in Shropshire. Jones Coachways operated local service work as well as contracts and holiday tours, including works services to Rists Wires and Cables in Newcastle-Under-Lyme. The coach is seen, however, in a sunny Shrewsbury at some time in 1991. (Photo Glenn Bubb)

A449 HJF had a long working life in North Staffordshire. New to Warringtons of Ilam in April 1984, this Plaxton Paramount-bodied Bedford YNT passed to Bernard Sutton of Reapsmoor and was his final coach. When Bernard retired, the vehicle and contracts passed to Wints Coaches of Butterton in 1993. Four years later it was on the move again to Taxi Co. and was based at their Cheadle depot. It wasn't repainted, the 'Wints' was removed and replaced by 'Taxi Co.', as seen here in Glebe Road, Cheadle. Despite its age, it was still in good order when sold by Taxi Co. and went to the Highlands of Scotland for further service with Rapsons until 2009. It is thought to still exist at Evie on the Isle of Orkney.

BGG 164S, a 12 m fifty-seven-seat Plaxton Supreme-bodied Volvo B58 new to Parks of Hamilton, was a well-used coach when it arrived with Countrywide Luxury Travel in 1999. The fleet was merged with that of Frank Booth, Swift Travel of Fenton, where it remained until that operator ceased following a traffic commissioners enquiry in 2003. It is seen heading back to Swift's base in Cheadle a year or so before then.

RIB 3524 typified the Clowes Coaches fleet in the early 2000s. An Auwaerter Neoplan 216H, new as C718 JTL, arrived from Robin Hood, Rudyard, in 1993 where it had been since it was two years old. It's seen here in Cheadle schools bus park looking good for a twenty-three-year-old coach.

New to Whittle's of Highley in May 1984 as ODN 601, A751 DUY was re-registered prior to sale to Wints Coaches at the end of 1988. The Wright Contour bodywork seated fifty-three and still carried its original livery with Wints. The turbocharged 500 power unit fitted to the Bedford YNT chassis was apparently a pig to start in cold weather.

PJI 5628, new as E352 EVH, joined the fleet of Malcolm Challinor of Talke by the start of the new millennium. The Van Hool T8 Alizée body was fitted to the rear-engine DAF SB3000DKV chassis – the more powerful of the two rear-engine DAF chassis. In this case, it is fitted with the 11.6-litre turbocharged engine. It's seen in Crewe returning to base following a morning contract journey around ten years ago.

WIL 3640, new in 1989 as F110 CCL, joined the Clowes of Longnor fleet in 2008, and was one of six Duple 425 integrals in the fleet, this particular one seating no fewer than sixty-one passengers. The Clowes operations reduced to one vehicle in 2014. WIL is seen here heading a line up of similar vehicles at the Barrow Moor depot in readiness for disposal at the auction sale that year.

A fine example of vehicle presentation is D159 VRP – an Alexander conversion of a Mercedes L608D, seating twenty passengers. A member of the Swift Mini Coaches fleet of Duke Street, Fenton, it came from PMT in 1988. Here it is parked in front of the author's Austin A55 MK II outside its base in 2001.

RIB 1080 from the Stanways fleet was a DAF SB2305 in the Duple 340 bodywork.
Underpowered with the 8.25-litre power unit, the coach was unpopular and spent a
lengthy period out of use. It's here, following its return to service around 2012, on a
Christmas pantomime trip to the New Victoria Theatre in Newcastle-Under-Lyme.
Withdrawal and export came soon afterwards.

E67 NVT, a classic design, is a Leyland Royal Tiger Doyen that was new to PMT as
E42 JRF and had arrived with Bennetts of Cranberry, via Dave Finney (D. A. Travel)
of Blurton, in 1997. Later re-registered to NIB 3264, then to A20 BNT, it was finally
withdrawn in 2015.

In a special commemorative BET livery in Cheadle High Street, KP54 LAO First Bus fleet number 32634 is a Volvo B7TL with seventy-four-seat Wright bodywork, new in 2005. Wintry weather makes for a dull day as it awaits passengers for Hanley.

6879 VT, the only double decker owned by Scraggs of Bucknall, was new as K710 ASC to Lothian Transport in 1992 but was a well-travelled bus by the time it arrived in Staffordshire from United Counties in 2009. Scraggs ran it for eight years, latterly on the weekday service 182 from Tean to Cheadle schools. It was finally withdrawn due to the high amount of vandal damage received.

Identity crisis! Former Crosville Bristol VR series 3 WDM 346R, carrying half a 'Rider' fleetname working for PMT, is about to depart the old Hanley Bus Station for Tean, via Cheadle, on the 232 service. It is driven by Mick Dudley in this mid-1990s view.

LWU 468V, one of few Bristol VRs to find favour with a Staffordshire independent, in this case Goldstraw of Cheadle and Leek, trading as Aimees' Taxi Co. bought this one from Devon General in 1999 and it kept its Stagecoach livery through its fairly short stay in the fleet. Its replacement for the 182 Tean–Cheadle schools' service was a T reg. Atlantean MCW from Go-ahead Northern the following year.

R726 EGD, D&G Coach and Bus fleet number 95, is a Mercedes 0810D Plaxton Beaver II B31F. It arrived from Travel Wright of Newark in 2007 and is pictured six years later on service in Newcastle Bus Station. D&G are one of the big success stories of deregulation in North Staffordshire and celebrated their twentieth anniversary in 2018.

Baker of Biddulph, once well known for their well turned out fleet of Green Coaches with RU registrations, became, for a period, a major operator of local bus services. T129 XVT, new to them in 1999, is seen a few years later in a damp Leek Bus Station on a now discontinued market day service. The Baker business later got tied up in the 'Island Fortitude'/King Long fiasco and was wound up in 2016, by which time bus service work had been abandoned.

E163 TWO is representative of the first generation of deregulation minibuses. New to National Welsh in April 1988 this twenty-seat Carlyle-bodied Freight Rover passed to Scraggs of Bucknall where, as seen here, it carries their 'Blue Buses' livery. Here it was employed on local services to Hanley. It's pleasing to report that over twenty years later Scraggs still provide local services in the area.

MIB 116, Copeland's Tours of Meir. This old established family firm are well known for their immaculate fleet of blue coaches. Local bus services were operated for a few years. Early members of the bus fleet included this and identical MIB 783, new as F49/45XPR, they arrived as ten-year-olds from Brighton and Hove in 1999. Both had Mercedes 811D chassis with Wadham Stringer bodies seating thirty-one. This view is taken at their Meir depot.

VNT 37S, a Bedford YLQ carrying Duple Dominant II C45F bodywork, was new to M & M of Kidderminster in 2/78. Its journey to North Staffordshire was as a three-year-old to join the fleet of Victoria Tours (Lymers) of Tean, where it gave fifteen years' service. On closure of the Lymers business it was bought by a local undertaker Syd Alcock of Cheadle, who operated from Lymers Garage. When Syd gave up PSV operations it passed briefly to Aimees where it was re-registered TXI 7007.

Another Aimee's coach was WRF 833X, a Ford R1114 Duple Dominant IV, which was new to Greatrex of Stafford but later returned to Staffordshire from M&H of Denbigh. It is seen at Aimee's Cheadle base C2002.

FUJ 901V, another ex-Whittle Group Bedford, this time a Dominant II YMT, passed to Colin Wint, photographed here looking very proud against his latest purchase in the mid-1980s. For many smaller operators, Bedfords were first choice for many years.

ENW 796Y, a late model Leyland Leopard PSU5G/5R, is a 12 m example with ZF six-speed manual gearbox – an option added to the Leopard range in order to give it more appeal to AEC customers when the Reliance was discontinued. Supplied new to Godson of Leeds, later passing to Steven's Birmingham, its Duple Dominant IV body was originally pink, later repainted cream and blue. It eventually arrived in Stoke-on-Trent with a Bentilee-based dance troupe. Out of use with them by Easter 2012 it was purchased as a possible preservation candidate, but was broken up for spares the following year.

Two unusual vehicles from the Longton-based Z Carz fleet, parked at their Spath outstation in 2012, are V690 EBC, a Cannon Hi-line C1000 with Leicester carriage builder C37F body, and D104 XAN (new as K1OLL), one of only two Scania K113 chassis to receive Plaxton Excalibur bodies. Both vehicles were used on school contracts around the Uttoxeter area.

Coach Aid of Stafford are primarily a PSV repair specialist but from time to time a courtesy vehicle is available for hire. On hire to Phil Smith in Spring 2009, XIL 5458 was a DAF MB230 new in 1988. It is seen carrying the original style Caetano Algarve bodywork new as F898 URP to Catterall, Southam.

Staffordshire County Council operated school services and sports/swimming contracts for around seventeen years from 1998 using a fleet of non-PSV yellow school buses. W426 VCH was an American-built rear-engine Bluebird. DX53 LFR at the rear was an example of the French-built Iveco Scolabus with Vehixel bodywork. With its front-mounted Iveco engine, brick-like bodywork, small wheels and odd driving position they were remarkably noisy and unpleasant vehicles to drive and had a tendency to understeer on any damp or greasy surface.

One of a pair of similar vehicles in the Bennetts of Cotes Heath fleet, KIW 8609 is a Volvo B10M 61 that was new in 1995 as B576 NJF with Plaxton Paramount body to Parry of Cheslyn Hay. By the late 1990s it was in service with Dunn Line, Nottingham, who in 2001 had it rebodied by Macedonian Motor Coach Industries as a sixty-five-seater to the style shown here. It arrived along with similar HIL 8286 (C122 ORM) at Bennetts in 2004. By the time this photo was taken in 2013, it had received the windscreen from a Mercedes minibus. Incredibly basic and poorly built, it was withdrawn by 2015.

MIB 783, Dennis Dart 985DL Plaxton Pointer B35F, was new to PMT in 1992 as J914 SRE, passing with sister J917 SRE to Copeland's in 2006/7. On withdrawal from Copeland's in 2015, both passed into preservation. 783 is seen here taking a break in Longton.

M67 HHB, number 12 in the D&G fleet, is a Dennis Dart with attractive Wright bodywork new to Red & White in 1995, from whom it was purchased in 2006. Seen here in the unmistakable 1960s surroundings of the old Hanley Bus Station. This was before D&G sold their North Staffs. operators to Wardles in 2011, only to return to the area two years later following Wardles sale to Arriva.

Originally registered G141 GOL, number 11 in the Wardle Transport fleet, RLZ 3218 was an early example of a Carlyle bodies Dennis Dart seen here operating service 85 to Newcastle-Under-Lyme Bus Station. After withdrawal by Wardles it is believed to have been sold for export.

TLZ 9426, not as first glance may suggest a Dennis Dart, is a rare example of a Marshall-bodied MAN 11.220, new in 1996 as N130 XEG. It arrived with Procter in 2007 and was a regular performer of the service 16 Hanley–Leek. The company closed unexpectedly in 2013, having operated route 16 since 1922.

BWY 709B, a fine Bedford VAL 14 with classic Duple Vega Major bodywork. It was new to Baddeley, Holmfirth, in 1963. Withdrawn by them in 1969, it passed to Bill Hall, Biddulph Moor, better known as an operator of AEC Reliance coaches. Bill kept it for three years before selling it to Butters of Childs Ercall, just over the border in Shropshire. The green of its original livery was retained, just the black centre panels receiving a coat of cream paint.

The only Bedford VAL operated by Smiths Tours of Waterhouses was this Plaxton-bodied VAL 70, UJU 931H, which saw less than a year's service before withdrawal in 1980. The stylish livery application was devised by Oliver Ball.

ACA 793L in the distinctive colours of BC Travel. The Ford R192 with Duple Viceroy Express C45F body arrived from Walker, Anderton, Cheshire, in May 1979. New to Williams & Davies of Wrexham, it, like many vehicles, had a fairly short stay with BC Travel, but remained in use after sale until 1988. (Photo Keith Stanton)

Mosswoods Direct Coal and Haulage of Wetley Rocks PSV operations passed, along with three operational coaches, to Berresford of Cheddleton in July 1978. The oldest vehicle in use was HAR 215C, a lovely short-length 1965 AEC Reliance 2MU4RA Plaxton Panorama I. It is parked at the rear of Berresfords Garage, still carrying its Comfy-Lux' fleetname and in full Mosswoods colours. It later received a partial repaint with more cream. Bringing up the rear is CTX 986C, a Byrnes of Leek AEC Reliance/Duple Commander dating from the same year.

RS Travel of Middlewich, Cheshire, were the operators of IIB 7460 – an unusual Van Hool-bodied Scania N112. The N112 chassis was usually the basis for double deck bodies, but this one, originally E219 FLD, was one of a batch of twenty-three new to Capital, West Drayton, in 1988, and by 2010 had arrived with RS Travel from Stanways of Kidsgrove. This view sees it on layover in the old Hanley Bus Station ready to work the 1445 X81 service (Wednesday/Friday only) to Winsford. RS Travel were bought out by the GHA Group in June 2011.

W371 ABD is a Dennis Dart/Marshall Capital. One of the most attractive bodies to be fitted to a Dart, this one was new to De Courcey of Coventry but was, for a time, part of the Dawson Rentals fleet, from whom it is on hire to Bakers of Biddulph in this Hanley Bus Station view dating from around 2009. It later went for further service with Darren Ridgway of Port Talbot and was eventually withdrawn in 2016.

S652 KJU is seen in Sneyd Green in service with Wardle Transport having been transferred from Arriva. The Volvo Olympian carries a late example of the Northern Counties Palatine II body and was new in 1998. It had left the fleet by 2015.

Scraggs of Bucknall 60 UVT, a Plaxton Primo Enterprise Plasma, had been new in 2005 to Central Connect as YX55 DSE. It arrived with Scraggs when five years old and is pictured in Hanley fairly soon after arrival. Obviously successful, it was later joined in the fleet by two similar machines.

G758 XRE was one of the final batch of double deckers delivered new to PMT. This coach-seated Cummins L10 engined Leyland Olympian was fitted with a five-speed gearbox and coach seats for use on the X20 Hanley to Crewe service. It is pictured on its first day in service in August 1989. Well liked and well built, most of the batch remained in service for well over twenty years.

Following closure of the Cheadle Bus Station in the mid-1990s, the operations moved to Brookhouse Industrial Estate on the western side of the town. It's here we find two of PMT's home-built 'Knype'-bodied Leyland Swifts – F312/5 REH – flanking a late model Bristol VRT3. The Knype wasn't a great success and, other than to PMT themselves, sales didn't happen. The VR was one of the coach-seated examples for use on larger distance services, and were very pleasant, fast vehicles to drive. The VR had a turbocharged Leyland 501 engine with a five-speed gearbox and high-speed rear axles, being capable of speeds well over 60 mph.

PMT was a big buyer of the
ill-fated Daimler Roadliner,
both in bus and coach versions.
KVT 168E is a Plaxton
Derwent-bodied Cummins
engine example seating fifty.
This posed view for company
publicity shows it advertising
the new 'Farebox' pay on
entry system trialled by several
operators in the late 1960s.

In the tranquil surroundings of Caverswall Square, with fire station, red phone box,
village stocks and oak tree for company, one of the first batch of Leyland Nationals
new to PMT, PVT 240L, sits awaiting passengers (of whom there were probably very
few) for its return journey to Longton and Hanley sometime around 1980.

Stanways operations have moved to across the border from Cheshire to Staffordshire and back several times. Their Optare Solo, DX07 WFA, is passing beneath the Kidsgrove–Crewe railway line, almost on the county border on service.

585 WKN was new as H16 KFC to Kings Ferry. This impressive Mercedes 0303/ Plaxton Paramount C53F was quite a rare machine. At one time owned by the author, but operated by Stanways, it was sold in March 2014 to Wints of Butterton. It's seen here the same month having just worked an afternoon Cheadle schools Whiston–Foxt–Ipstones tendered 234 (school days only) service. The backdrop for the photo is Bottom House and the main Ashbourne–Leek A523 road. Withdrawn in summer 2016, it was broken up on site for spares.

F33 ENF. New to the Shearings Group this rather attractive Cummins-powered Leyland Tiger Alexander 'N' Type fitted in well with the Stanway fleet. At one time registered JSK 978, the bus had also served with Arriva and Heartlands from whom it was purchased along with similar F39, F52 ENF in 2010. After five years or so it was sold for further use to Walters of Oxfordshire. It is believed to still exist in preservation.

LUI 9030 is a tidy example of the ever-popular Mercedes 0814 Plaxton Cheetah thirty-three-seat coach. Freshly painted in Stanways colours it had received a fairly major body overhaul before entering service. It is seen here raised in the air on the Hywemas ready for its planned maintenance inspection.

Smiths of Waterhouses had recently sold out when this photograph was taken in 1981, at the rear of Berresfords Garage in Cheddleton. NFM 689E, a Bedford VAM 70 with Plaxton Panorama II body, had arrived from Crosville less than two years previously but was deemed of no further use by Berresfords and was scrapped. (Photo Martyn Hearson)

Thomsons Tours of New Park Garage, Trentham, kept a small modern fleet of lightweight coaches throughout the sixties and seventies. Making a change from the more usual Duple- and Plaxton-bodied coaches, HWP 414N, a Ford R1114, carried an example of the Caetano Estoril II body (Portuguese built but imported by Alf Moseley). It arrived with Thomsons as a three-year-old in April 1978 from Regent of Redditch. (Photo R. Folwell)

Bennetts of Cranberry operated for many years in this distinctive livery before changing to the purple they use today. B224 WEU, a Leyland Tiger/Duple Laser II, joined the fleet from Collinson of Stonehouse in 1995. It is working a school journey as it crosses the Stone–Colwich section of the West Coast Main Line adjacent to the now demolished Meaford Crossing signal box in 2001.

VAB 434R, a Bedford YLQ Duple Dominant C45F, was new to Halford of Kempsey and had been added to the fleet of Andrew Hall (Hamps Valley Coaches) of Benty Grange Lane, Winkhill, in February 1983. It had come from the fleet of Eyre (Robin Hood) of Rushton Spencer, who acquired the coach when it was almost new. Hamps Valley kept the coach for many years, and it's seen here with the proprietor at the wheel at the Stafford County Showground in the mid-1990s.

VRF 186L is a Bedford YRQ Plaxton Panorama Elite Express C45F. New to Warringtons of Ilam under the bus grant scheme, this little Bedford gave ten years' service before passing to H. Williams of Storton-by-Stow, who operated it in Warringtoms colours, as seen here in this view from the mid-1980s taken in Gainsborough. (Photo Sturton and Stow Historic Society, Lincolnshire)

Two more typical Fords from the Thomsons fleet, DWE 508H and NXJ 5H, both carry the original style Plaxton Panorama Elite body on the 11 metre R226 chassis. DWE arrived as a one-year-old from Sims, Sheffield, NXJ arrived a year later from Finglands, Manchester. (Photo R. Folwell)

Plenty of interest in this 1980 view on the forecourt at Berresfords. Centre stage is taken by CYD 234J, a lovely 10 m AEC Reliance 6MU4R Plaxton Panorama Elite II from the Mosswoods (County-Lux) fleet who'd purchased it in 1973 from Pearce, Darch & Wilcox, Martock. (Photo Martyn Hearson)

SEL 676H was a vehicle that moved between the related fleets of Downs (Waltonian) of Stone and Stanways during the 1980s. New to Excelsior, it was a Ford R192 Plaxton Panorama Elite I and carried a different livery application on each side. (Photo Telford Bus Group).

Ascending Lime Kiln Bank, Bucknall, en route to Hanley in this 1986 view, PCH 418L, new to Trent Motor Traction, was one of only three Bristol vehicles to be operated by the Berresford Group. New to Trent, this Leyland 680 engined RE with attractive ECW bodywork had been purchased from Redline earlier in the year. Following takeover by PMT, it was the only Berresford vehicle to be painted into red/yellow livery.

JJZ 5289, a Wardle Travel Dennis Dart, leaves Hanley behind as it travels along the busy thoroughfare of Victoria Road, Fenton, Lightwood via Longton in 2012.

A506 FSS, from the Glovers of Ashbourne fleet, was a regular performer on school contracts and private hire work in the Uttoxeter area. Bought out of service from Glovers in June 2009 by the author, it's seen in Cheadle, en route to Alf Tunstall Bus Rally at Froghall Station. Fully restored into original Northern Scottish livery, the Dennis Lancet/Alexander P Type Perkins V8-540 has recently changed ownership for continued preservation by George McKechnie.

V370 KLG, First Bus fleet number 41070, is a Marshall Dennis Dart SLF new to Chester and is seen in a busy Leek Bus Station one Wednesday morning early in 2014.

ONY 4M, FT Stubbs, Williamson Street, Tunstall. An old, established garage and coach operator who sold the PSV side of the business along with three coaches to Berresfords in 1978. ONY was a Ford R226 Duple Dominant C53F, bought as a one-year-old in 1975 from Thomas, Clydach Vale. The coach later received Berresfords Ayres Red/Ivory and was scrapped on site in 1987. Stubbs reappeared as a coach operator for a period from the late 1980s.

438 CBF was an early example of a Bedford VAS1 fitted with the Bedford 300 cu. in. diesel engine. It was new to Victoria Tours (Lymers) of Tean in 1962, where it remained for nineteen years before passing to Roy Cooper of Elkstone. By the mid-1980s it had left Roy Cooper to join the small operation of Hugh Plimmer in Cheadle. After sale by Plimmers it became a mobile home in the Meir area of Stoke-on-Trent, eventually meeting its end at a Cheadle scrapyard when around thirty-five years old. Its registration number, however, lives on, being bought from the scrap by the driver who collected the coach from Duple when new, undertaker and coach operator, the late Sydney T. Alcock of Cheadle.

A rarely seen type of vehicle in the Stoke-on-Trent area was the Bristol MW. This attractively liveried ECW coach-bodied example, HDV 638E, joined the BC Travel fleet of Bill Stanton from Western National in June 1978. Based at that time in Tean, HDV only lasted with BC Travel until the following May when it passed to St Margaret's School, Aigburth, via Martins Bus & Coach Sales of Middlewich. The bus survives in preservation in Royal Blue livery.

A later member of the BC Travel fleet, OAX 28R, a Ford R1114 Caetano Estoril II, arrived along with similar NKO 33P from Rogers of Langside in October 1980. The coach had been new to Thomas, Clydach Vale, in August 1976, and passed from BC Travel when the company closed at the end of 1983 to Alpha Dentonian, of Manchester, where it was repainted white with tan/brown stripes. (Photo K. Stanton)

M197 UAN is an unusual Berkhoff-bodied Dennis Lance with Paragon Travel, Uttoxeter. It was one of a batch new to Speedlink which had also seen service with McKindless of Wishaw. It is fully lettered for the company's 428 service to Lichfield via Abbotts Bromley, from where it had just arrived. It's seen in Uttoxeter Bus Station in 2010. The vehicle wasn't a success and spent lengthy periods off the road.

Thirty years earlier than the previous photo, and in more or less the same location, a Green Bus Services Leyland Tiger-Cub East Lancashire B44F waits on its allocated stand ready to depart on basically the same service as the Lance pictured above, its journey taking in the scenic village of Abbotts Bromley en route. New in 1964, the Tiger-Cub was typical of the elderly Leyland-based fleet of Warstone Motors (Green Bus Services) of Great Wyrley, near Cannock.

Resplendent in Stonier's distinctive Pippin Red/Arundel Lilac livery, JPA 176K, former Green Line RP76, was posed on the forecourt of Berresfords Garage prior to entering service in August 1980. Several of these fine vehicles entered service within the Berresfords Group, further examples being purchased until 1986. Later reseated with bus seats they were fast, reliable buses that were very popular with drivers and passengers alike. The AEC Reliance chassis had the AH691 power unit, power steering and five-speed semi-automatic gearbox. The Park Royal body was unique to this batch of vehicles, which numbered ninety in total. (Photo Martyn Hearson)

Working a p.m. journey on the Endon schools–Brown Edge service, on hire to Knotty Bus, ESC 844S was a very tidy Seddon Pennine VII with manual gearbox and Gardner 6HLXB engine topped with Alexander classic Y Type bodywork. The 'Handy Bus' fleet of Matthews Motors was based just outside Newcastle and operated services with a fleet consisting mainly of minibuses.

H153 DJU was the first Dennis Javelin purchased by Warringtons of Ilam after Bedfords ceased to be available. Looking immaculate, despite being nearly twenty years old in this view, its Plaxton Paramount III body carries the traditional fleet colours of Ayres red/cream/black. The Javelin was a natural successor to the Bedford and the type is well respected at Warringtons, being economical and reliable in service. Cheadle schools is the location for this photo.

On the ramps at Boydons Winkhill Garage, former London County TD9 Leyland Tiger/Duple Dominant IV Express was one of the last vehicles to be purchased by Boydons before the company closed in 2006. It arrived from Mike James, Invincible Coaches, Tamworth. It was sold without MOT at the dispersal sale in March 2007, presumably for scrap.

L501 YRY was not a Plaxton Paramount but a Leicester Carriage Builders-bodied
Volvo B10M. Bennetts got good service from this unusual coach, purchasing it from
West Glamorgan County Council in 2001. It was re-registered at various times to
VOV 723 and A15 BNT and was still active in 2017.

An older vehicle from the Bennetts fleet, XJG 812V was a 12 m Leyland Leopard/
Duple Dominant II that had been new to East Kent but came from Ivor J. Lucas of
Kingsley in 1993, where it had been for three years. Another long-lived vehicle with
Bennetts, it was finally retired in 2004.

YDZ 3458, new as A226 VWO, was an East Lancashire rebodied Leyland Tiger. It was new to Rhonda but arrived in Staffordshire with RML Travel, via Road Car and Nu-Venture of Maidstone. It is pictured passing the now demolished Smithfield public house in Blythe Bridge in 2008. Later repainted red with a gold roof the bus gave around three more years' service.

One of the many odd vehicles to find its way into the privatised PMT fleet was HHJ 374Y, a Leyland Tiger Alexander TE Type. Numbered STL 297 in the fleet, it arrived from Brewers in 1997 and was based at Newcastle, where it's pictured in the old bus station. It lasted around three years in the fleet before disposal.

G114 ENV. Stylish Duple 300 bus bodywork is mounted on a Volvo B10M chassis and was a member of the combined JST/Transport Direct fleet for use on school's work around the Uttoxeter area. Its normal run served Leigh and the Bents. It was new to Northampton. It had also seen service with First in Leicester and Midland Red, in the Worcester area, before arriving with JST via Premiere Coaches from the East Midlands.

The immaculate fleet of Paul's Coaches still includes this thirty-three-year-old Leyland Tiger Plaxton Derwent. New to the Ministry of Defence as 82KF09 it joined the Paul's fleet from Edward Thomas, West Ewell, in 2016 after fifteen years with Thomas. Re-registered to D458 ENV in 1997 while with the Driving Standards Agency, its seventy-seat capacity makes it a useful school bus.

PMT's Daimler Roadliners, like many elsewhere, had notoriously short service lives, most being withdrawn at seven years old. Plaxton Derwent-bodied WEH 133G found further use as an (im)mobile shop at Farthing Corner Services on the M2 in Kent, where I photographed it alongside my Sunbeam Rapier in September 1980. Last taxed in 1984 according to DVLA records, I assume it has long since been scrapped.

An interesting and unique batch of buses to join the Berresford Group in 1981 were TDK540/1J, 542–6 9K AEC Swift/Pennine B40D, built to the order of Rochdale Corporation. Bargain buys, 541–6 entered service with the first and last of the batch retained for spares. Very reliable in service, and pleasant to drive, 543 typifies the batch in this 1983 view in Glebe Street, Stoke-on-Trent.

One of PMT's first batch of Alexander Y Type AEC Reliances. KVT 183E speeds along an empty A500 'D' road as seen from Glebe Street in 1980. Some of the batch received bus livery in later years but all had left the fleet by 1982.

BC Travel JKK 181E is pictured at PMT's Stoke Garage shortly before withdrawal in 1983. 'Jake' as it was known had arrived from the fleet of Graham Durber of Talke in January 1980, where it had been for two years since arriving from Hants & Dorset. The Willowbrook-bodied Leyland Panther was sold for scrap in November 1983.

909 EUM. A splendid Roe-bodied Leyland Titan PD3A/1 arrived at Stonier from Hardwick of Scarborough in July 1972 and served for nearly eight years. This view, dating from the mid-1970s, sees it adjacent to Stonier's Goldenhill premises, which were vacated in 1980.

Variety at Biddulph depot in the Walley Street premises shared by PMT and Crosville. 223 NAE, new to Bristol Omnibus, is a Bristol Lodekka FLF 6G and is hiding behind ex-North Western Road AEC Renown/Park Royal VDB 976, on Daimler Fleetline/ Alexander FJA 211D in this 1976 view.

Gardner smoke. An ex-South Yorkshire Daimler Fleetline/Alexander coughs into life one morning in early 1986 at Stonier's Tunstall depot on Parsonage Street, with an unwell Pennine-bodied AEC Swift to keep it company. The smoke from a Gardner engine on cold start was of the most acrid, eye-watering type, akin to rubbing a raw onion against your eyeballs!

An independent Lodekka. Lymers, Victoria Tours of Tean, were the owners of HLJ 221D, an FLB6B, originally Bristol engined, but by this point repowered with a Garner 6LW. It arrived from Hants & Dorset in December 1981, where it had been fleet number 1247 and carried NBC Poppy Red livery throughout its stay with Lymers. Returning to the garage in June 1985, it has just dropped off the last of its school passengers, having worked the 182 service from Cheadle with another two years' service ahead of it. It was retired at the end of the summer in 1987. It is believed to have been sold on for use as a Driver Trainer.

Stoddards of Cheadle got good service from this Bova Europa 387 STT. New as A805 JAY, it arrived in the fleet as a two-year-old in 1986. This photo shows it on tour in Amsterdam, driven by John Hodgson in the late 1980s. (Photo Franz Angevaare)

Same bus with the same driver but around twenty-five years later, by which time it was the oldest vehicle in the Stoddard fleet and had been relegated to school bus duties. In this Cheadle school bus park view it is now wearing an approximation of Stoddards later blue/silver livery. John positions the coach ready for its journey to Grindon via Waterhouses.

Plaxton Paramount 3500 MK I bodywork is carried by this Leyland Tiger from the Boydon of Winkhill fleet. VIB 6165 had joined the fleet as a twelve-year-old in 1995 from Gelsthorpe of Mansfield. New as BAJ 632Y, it had also carried 540 CCY and SWN 885Y. Fitted with forty-nine well-spaced seats, it served the company until closure and was sold with current PSV MOT in the March 2007 auction.

MBC 218V – a Bedford YMT with distinctive Unicar bodywork. This view shows it just after purchase, in 1993, by the late Joe Lightfoot, who traded for a period as Lightfoot Leisure. The coach arrived from Brough of Norton, who traded as Compass Travel, but still carried the livery of original operator Woods of Leicester. It replaced KVD 456P on AEC Reliance/Duple C49FT with Joe Lightfoot. It was later repainted in an unusual livery of pale green/yellow/mauve.

Procter's Coaches, by this time based at Dewsbury Road, Fenton, were the owners of this comparatively rare short length Bova FHD 10-340, TLZ 2656. New in 1999 as T759 JYB, it arrived from Helyer, Fareham, in 2006 as a luxuriously specified thirty-six-seater executive coach. Procter's sadly and unexpectedly closed the doors in 2013 after over eighty years of trading.

BX14 KRV, an ex-demonstrator King Long XMQ 6127Y, joined the Aimee's fleet in April 2016 from the fleet of Harrington's Coaches (Bakers), Knypersley. Unusually specified as a dual-entrance coach, it is regularly used on both schools and private hire work.

An immaculately presented Leyland Tiger/Van Hool from the Copeland's fleet MIB 970 had arrived from Sunberry of Shepperton in 2003. Already some twenty years old, the coach was treated as normal with Copeland's to a full overhaul before entering service. Named *Lady Rosemary II* and re-registered from NYS 58Y, it was finally withdrawn at thirty-two years old at the end of the school year in 2015.

A long-time member of the fleet of George Edwards of Wrexham, L537 EHD arrived at JST of Uttoxeter in February 2015 from Lakeside of Ellesmere. The Van Hool body seated fifty-seven and was mated to the powerful 11.6-litre engine DAF SB3000 chassis with four-over-four manual gearbox. This smooth driving coach was withdrawn after less than five months' service, passing to the associated operations of Chester Coaches who ran from a farmyard on the outskirts of that city.

A 1980 line up at PMT's Clough Street Hanley depot sees examples of three different batches of Leyland Atlantean PDR1 dating from 1959–1962. All are fitted with low-height MCW bodywork. 767 EVT (second in line) was numerically the second Atlantean delivered to PMT. These were well liked long-serving vehicles, yet withdrawal and scrapping was imminent. Similar 766 EVT, however, survives with the Potteries Omnibus Preservation Society.

Three years on from the above photo and the first batch of Leyland Olympians for PMT are lined up in the same place as the Atlanteans above. A733–7 GFA represent the first five of the fifteen-string batch. Some of the batch survived for twenty years and one of their number, 747 is preserved in red/yellow by Paul Pearson former POPS secretary.

XEH 252M was the only short National from the PMT fleet to receive red/yellow livery. It was specifically painted for use on former Berresford routes following sale of that company to PMT in May 1987. It is pictured here at Cellarhead in the summer of 1987 ready to take up service.

WT58 SOT was an appropriate registration for this Wardle Travel Optare Versa V1100. It had luxury specification with thirty-eight leather high-backed seats and laminate flooring. Delivered new in 2008, the 'Plumline' brand was an attempt to provide a higher quality of bus service of the Hanley–Blurton corridor. Initially carrying this all-over deep plum livery, the bus was later repainted into a cream-based livery.

Transport Direct of Bramshall acquired this Plaxton Beaver II-bodied Mercedes 0814D B28FL in the summer of 2017 from a Scottish operator. KF52 UAD was new to Nottingham City Council for disabled transport. It is pictured here in the village of Lower Leigh one icy morning in December 2017, working a schools' contract to Windsor Park School in Uttoxeter.

A wintry Cheadle High Street in 2011 sees Clowes of Longnor K867 ODY, a Mercedes 709D/Alexander B25F, attempting to pick up on the bus stop in High Street on service 234 to Leek, via Ipstones. The vehicle had come from Stagecoach South in 2002 and gave over ten years' service in the arduous lanes of the Staffordshire Moorlands.

JST International Optare Solo X165 NWR, operating the Staffordshire County Council tendered Cheadle town service in 2015. The Solo had arrived from Stott, Milnbridge, in 2013 and retained their livery throughout its three-year stay. Ticketing equipment was of a very basic level, a 'speed' setright on the cab floor with a biscuit tin for the takings!

X293 FFA, First bus 40023, is an Optare Solo B27F, which was new in 2000 as one of PMT's third batch of similar vehicles. It is pictured here around ten years old and still looking very smart in Hanley, with the BBC Radio Stoke building and war memorial in the background. The area is now pedestrianised in the city's latest attempt to cause confusion to anyone trying to drive through it.

LUJ 252F, a delightful petrol engine Bedford VAM3/Duple Viceroy C45F, was new to Salopia of Whitchurch in April 1968. It was acquired by the Burnwoodairs Dance Troupe of Chell Heath after service with Blands of Cottesmore. Blands caramel paint was brightened up with a coat of orange and the coach is pictured one Saturday morning, around 1982, in Chell Heath. Eventually repainted blue, it survived until 1988.

Another dance troupe bus, 553 GXX had been new to Timpson, but by 1977/78 had settled for a quieter life with the 'Wulston Reyelles' from Wolstanton, around 6 miles from where the photo was taken in Clough Hall Road Kidsgrove. The fine Harrington Grenadier-bodied AEC Reliance had also served with an operator named Whites Coaches.

JRF 990K, a Ford R192 Duple Viceroy Express with Leon's Coaches of Stafford is pictured near the end of its life in 1992. New to Austin (Happy Days), Woodseaves, it had been with Leon's since November 1979. Leon Douglas had started as a taxi operator with a fleet of Ford Zephyr MK III cars. Known for their reliable, economic service, Fords made a natural choice as PSVs.

W. Jeffreys of Goldenhill claimed to have been transport providers since the mid-nineteenth century and at one time operated a fleet of modern coaches mostly bought new. By the 1970s, the heyday of coach travel was in decline, and the once sparkling fleet of brown/cream coaches were employed mainly on the transport of the handicapped, pensioners and church groups, and often appeared dull and uncared for. 180 YMA, a typical member of the (by that time) all-Bedford fleet, had arrived when it was seven years old from Lomas, Macclesfield. It was a Bedford SB3 Duple Bella Vega seating forty-one and was new in 1963. Pictured here outside the ramshackle Charlotte Street garage, it was sold to Ivor J. Lucas when Jeffreys closed at the start of the 1980s and the area was redeveloped.

BNP 11W, a 12 m Volvo B58-61/Caetano Alpha C57F, had joined the Leon's of Stafford fleet in 1984 and is seen at rest at around eight or nine years later. Leon's are well known today for their high-class fleet of executive coaches providing UK and European holiday travel, as well as schools and college services.

Two mid-1990s members of the 'Executive Travel' fleet from Heron Cross, looking about as far removed from anything executive as possible, are ONA 7H – a rare survivor of the Bedford VAM70/Plaxton Panorama Elite – and PKE 185W – a Bedford YMT Duple Dominant II, ex-Maidstone and still in their colours. ONA was later re-registered to MBF 353H and survived long enough to see the name of the operations changed to 'Ambassador' in 1997. It was still on fleet strength in 2000 but unused.

Knotty Bus number 2, PPH 431R, AEC Reliance 6U2R/Plaxton C53F was purchased in 1988. By 1990 it carried the grey/orange colours of associated operator Melvyn Jones (LMS Travel), but by 1991 had returned to the main Knotty fleet. After a period out of use, it was re-seated, re-engined with an AH 691 unit in place of the original AH 760 and repainted into a hybrid livery of black/white, but retained the grey window surrounds and roof.

AOI 3429 is an example of the Bedford YMT with Van Hool 300 series bodywork. The only other PSV to receive LMS Travel livery, it saw little use and was sold in 1991 for further service.

MVT 452V was the final new purchase by Stoddards of Cheadle. It was a very basic specification Bedford SB5/Duple Dominant C41F with a manual door. It's seen here in the early 1990s outside Cheadle Library, adjacent to Greenhill Garage, Stoddard base. It gave a full twenty-one years of service before withdrawal in July 2001.

'You are travelling Overland, majestically' so read the elegant gold leaf wording above the windscreen on the interior of PCK 951K, a Bedford SB5 Plaxton Panorama IV C41F – a long time member of the Lymers of Tean fleet. It arrived with them in January 1976 from Everett, Atterby. In October 1989 it moved a couple of miles up the road to Stoddards of Cheadle, where it lasted until 1993. Pictured here on the A5 at Gailey, it was about to make a very long journey overland and sea in 'kit' form to Pakistan, thanks to Martin Perry of Bromyard.

Another Bedford SB5 to spend some time with Stoddards of Cheadle. SFP 829X is pictured here in Leek Bus Station working part of the network of rural bus services run by its original owner, Warringtons from Ilam. Unusually sporting a Bristol Dome, and full destination equipment along with power door, it had been bought under the bus grant scheme. It is believed to still exist in the Netherlands.

Smiths Tours of Waterhouses operated this Bedford SB/Harrington Crusader III, BVO 25C. Bought from Barton of Chilwell in October 1974, it was a regular vehicle for use on local service work around the villages between Leek and Ashbourn; its electrically operated sliding door being very useful on such duties. By 1977 it had moved to South Wales.

Bowkers of Kidsgrove ceased operations at the end of 2008. One of the final vehicles operated was A987 POD, a Bedford YNT Plaxton Paramount C53F with Cummins engine. New to Turner of Chumleigh in Devon, it was quite an elderly vehicle when it arrived in Staffordshire. On withdrawal I bought the coach and later sold it for conversion to a car transporter.

This rather attractive Bristol LHS/Plaxton Supreme thirty-five-seater joined the Plimmer of Cheadle fleet in May 1989 from Harris of Catshill. TIA 6965 had been new to Baker, Biddulph, as LBF 701P in August 1975, and also worked for Eagle of Bristol from May 1979, and Wickson of Clay by the mid-1980s. Repainted into this attractive primrose/dark green livery, it's at Plimmer's rural depot shortly after arrival. It lasted four years before sale to Searle of Thornhaugh.

Bassetts Coachways of Tittensor bought this Leyland Tiger/ Plaxton Supreme V from Wrekin Coachways of Oakengates in 1999. New to Robinson, Great Harwood, as LEC 197X, it retained this dark blue livery when with Bassetts. It is seen here on a Stone school contract in 2002 shortly before Bassetts abandoned PSV operations. After this the coach was sold for further service in Scotland. It is currently preserved by Andy Fudge and wears full Bassetts blue/grey colours.

Phil Lawrence operated this Ford R1114 Plaxton Supreme IV during the mid-1990s. Believed to have been new to Copeland's as ORF 888W, it was used on various school contracts and is pictured in the Knotty Bus yard at Chesterton.

The longest serving vehicle with Knotty was KVE 909P, bought from Premier Travel in 1989 looking scruffy and threadbare inside. Following a re-trim and coat of paint it proved to be an excellent buy. It is seen heading up Smallthorne Bank, driven by the author, heading for Burslem and Tunstall on the Saturdays-only Staffordshire Bus tendered service from Ball Green, sometime in 1991. During its stay at Knotty, KVE carried a few different liveries, this being its first. (Photo Martyn Hearson)

NWO 61R, a Bedford YMT/ Plaxton C53F new to Capital, Cwmbran, was pictured at Copeland's depot in Meir, operated by Countryside (Frank Booth) in 1999. It had been bought from Lubinski & Johnson of Longton the previous year.